Using Art in Sunday Worship

Eileen Gurak

RESOURCE PUBLICATIONS, INC.
San Jose, California

Editorial director: Kenneth Guentert
Managing editor: Kathi Drolet
Copy editor: Elizabeth J. Asborno
Art director: Terri Ysseldyke-All
Illustrations: Jean Snow

Reprint Department
Resource Publications, Inc.
160 E. Virginia Street, #290
San Jose, CA 95112-5848

Library of Congress Cataloging in Publication Data

Gurak, Eileen, 1946-
    Using art in Sunday worship / Eileen Gurak.
        p.   cm.
    Includes bibliographical references (p.)
    ISBN 0-89390-186-5
    1. Catholic Church and art.   2. Catholic Church —
Liturgical objects.   3. Colors, Liturgical.   I. Title.
    N72.R4G87   1990
    264'.02 — dc20   90-8949

Contents

PART II

Preface

This book has grown out of a need I have perceived as I have given talks on art and environment in liturgy based on the bishops' statement, *Environment and Art in Catholic Worship*. These ideas first appeared seven years ago in the form of a handout, and I have continued to refine them since then. I speak to people on parish liturgy teams who are responsible for designing the environment for the seasonal liturgical celebrations in their parish. My goal is to offer theological theory and practical application.

I soon learned that many people were not familiar with the standard vocabulary of liturgy, so an explanation of terms has proven helpful. Much of *Environment and Art in Catholic Worship* is directed toward the building and renovating of liturgical space. The people attending my workshops are looking for guidelines for the environment of the Sunday celebration. I have compiled guidelines along with practical suggestions on how to implement them. Since I am speaking about the discipline of art, a distinction needs to be made between sacred art in general and the special requirements of liturgical art. I have included design principles and patterns to help people create a prayerful, beautiful, and sound liturgical season.

The courses at the Liturgy Institute of Chicago have provided me with deeper insights into the ramifications of my earlier studies of the needs of the environment and art. Also they have made me more aware of how symbols are not limited to objects but include gesture and ritual action as well. I have applied these principles to the environment and included these ideas in this book.

The following is a key to the abbreviations found in the text notes. The publication information on these can be found in the bibliography.

C.S.L. - *Constitution on the Sacred Liturgy*

E.A.C.W. - *Environment and Art in Catholic Worship*

G.I.R.M. - *General Instruction of the Roman Missal*

I.F.R. - *Introduction of the Funeral Rite*

Using Art in
Sunday Worship

Part I

Liturgy

To understand how art can serve liturgy requires a close look at liturgy. Liturgy defies a single definition; it is multi-faceted like a diamond.

> In the liturgy, by means of signs perceptible to the senses, human sanctification is signified and brought about in ways proper to each of these signs; in the liturgy the whole public worship is performed by the Mystical Body of Jesus Christ, that is, by the Head and His members (C.S.L. #7).

Liturgy is the public worship of the Church.

Liturgy is the work of the Church.

Liturgy is the experience of ourselves as the people of God, the Church, and the experience of the mystery of God (E.A.C.W. #12).

Liturgy is the baptized faithful gathered around word and sacrament.

Liturgy is pageantry and movement; there are elements of dance and drama within the liturgy that demand graceful execution.

Liturgy requires time and that time must be given graciously by all—the presider, the liturgical ministers, and the assembly—so that the liturgy may unfold in an unhurried manner.

Liturgy has a flow and rhythm; great care must be taken that it does not become parts strung together.

Liturgy has a balance between the verbal and non-verbal, between sounds and silence, between spoken words and music, which must be respected (E.A.C.W. #25).

How we do liturgy—the dignity with which we move, the care with which we handle our sacred objects, the enthusiasm we put into our singing, and the sensualness we use to create our sacred space—tells one another about our God. We are sharing our faith.

Sacred Art and Liturgical Art

God does not need liturgy, people do, and people have only their own arts and styles of expression with which to celebrate (E.A.C.W. #4).

Like the two leaves of a seedling plant, liturgy and art have their unseen roots deep in the mystery of God. Art and worship both dwell in the realm of symbol; both speak to the soul of mystery, life and God. An important distinction needs to be made between sacred art in general and art that lends itself to liturgy and can be considered liturgical art. The other categories of sacred art have different functions, most of which are not appropriate to the needs of liturgy.

Devotional Art

The purpose of devotional art is to inspire and foster private or personal piety. Most of the pictures and statues familiar to us fall into this category. Works of devotional art are important to our spiritual life. Because of its personal nature, devotional art does not lend itself well to liturgy's communal character in the western church.

Educational Art

The purpose of education art is to teach about the life of Christ and Church doctrine. Much of the art of the Middle Ages is educational art as well as devotional art. Though many of these art works were used in the liturgy, their purpose was to teach. The murals and stained glass windows were the Bible for the believer who could not read. Educational art continues to have an important place in our textbooks and classrooms. This is not considered liturgical art because it is not the purpose of liturgy to educate people. Liturgy is designed to help people experience the mystery of Christ present among his people.

Prophetic Art

This art form makes a person uncomfortable. It points a finger at a situation that should be changed or should not be forgotten. Prophetic art is indispensable in challenging the believer but cannot be considered liturgical art. Though at times the worship environment may have a stark and upsetting feel similar to prophetic art, it must not draw attention to its individual message.

Liturgical Art

Liturgical art is art at the service of the liturgy. It is not art for art's sake and doesn't call attention to itself. Liturgical art's purpose is to enhance and give dignity to the ritual and movement. This art helps to immerse the community into the Paschal Mystery, the dying and rising of Jesus. It creates an environment that helps everyone experience the liturgical season—be it the seriousness of Lent or the exuberance of Easter.

Liturgical art appeals to the senses! We taste it, we smell it, we see it, we feel it, we hear it. Liturgical art takes the everyday things of life—bread, wine, eating, drinking, table, water, bathing, oil, book, candle, light, darkness, clothing, and people—and transforms them to speak of the profound. Liturgical art lives in the tension between a sense of mystery and awe and objects/actions that are commonplace. An object/action should not be so commonplace that the sense of awe is missing, nor should its awesomeness be so strong that its everyday nature is lost.

Symbols

Liturgy dwells in the realm of symbols, which are multi-level realities that speak of mysteries too profound to be "understood" in any other way. With a symbol, "you get more than you see." Symbols are everyday objects/actions that, besides containing an element of what they are or do, point to a greater reality. For this reason the eucharistic bread and wine should look like real food (G.I.R.M. #283) so they can point to the greater reality of being fed and strengthened by our God with sustenance for the journey of life. There should be the sharing of one loaf (G.I.R.M. #3) so that it may speak of unity. There should be the eye contact between the eucharistic minister and the communicant to speak the strong message of community and reconciliation.

Symbols are actions as well as objects: "take and eat," "take and drink," and "whenever you *gather* in my name." This shifts the emphasis from the object of bread and the object of wine to the action of breaking, pouring, and sharing of communion. This has a far-reaching effect on what is done at liturgy and how it is done.

> Renewal requires the opening of our symbols, especially the fundamental ones of bread and wine, water, oil, the laying on of hands, until we can experience all of them as authentic and appreciate their symbolic value (E.A.C.W. #15).

This demands a *maximum* use of symbols: lots of water for baptism so the candidates get wet; full gesture during the Eucharistic Prayer; oil that is poured on for anointing. Our symbols speak to us of our God and we have a maximum God! Pragmatic, convenient, and minimal symbols suggest a parsimonious God. The God of scripture and Christian tradition is generous and incomprehensible; those are qualities demanding a full and generous use of symbols.

Symbols work on the intuitive level of understanding. When something is understood on the intuitive level, it is "known" although a person would be at a loss to explain it. The intuitive level is the level of conversion. We don't believe in God because we were taught to; we believe because somehow we "know" God. This level is addressed through the senses: sight, sound, smell, touch. Scripture and the incarnation show a very sensual God, who speaks in poetry and parables. The language of liturgy is the language of symbol, ritual action, the intuitive, poetry, and the senses.

Liturgy is total, and therefore must be much more than a merely rational or intellectual exercise. In view of our culture's emphasis on reason, it is critically important for the Church to reemphasize a more total approach to the human person by opening up and developing the non-rational elements of the liturgical celebration: the concern for feelings of conversion, support, joy, repentance, trust, love, memory, movement, gesture, wonder (E.A.C.W. #35).

Bread and Wine

The bread and wine are food and should have the appearance of such (G.I.R.M. #283). A sense of mystery is created by how this food is handled, the size and beauty of the plate and cup they are placed in, and where they are placed on the altar. This cup and plate belong to everyone, and food that is shared in common is placed in the center of the table. Therefore the cup and plate should be in the center of the altar (furthest from the priest) with the Sacramentary (the priest's missal) between him and the gifts. In this way we say these gifts, this bread and wine, belong to all.

In order to call attention to these central symbols and as a sign of the unity that they "make real," it is desirable to use only one large bread plate and either one large chalice or one large flagon (E.A.C.W. #96). During the singing of the Lamb of God, the bread should be broken and placed on smaller plates; also at this time the wine is poured into cups for communion. All this speaks visually and intuitively of the importance of unity. Our use of symbols and gesture forms us into the people of God.

Altar

> The altar, the holy table, should be the most noble, the
> most beautifully designed and constructed table the com-
> munity can provide (E.A.C.W. #71).

The altar is a table and as such should be treated with dignity. Because the altar is not a bulletin board, we have come
to realize that an antependium with words, symbols, or pictures does not belong hanging on the front of the altar. All
cloths used on the altar should cover it as they would a table:
fully to the floor or over the top with a drop, or as a runner
from side to side or front to back. Because color evokes emotions and texture expresses mood, it is important that the
color and texture capture the liturgical season. This requires
delving into how a season feels and knowing what colors and
textures express that. Layers of runners used over fuller cloths
allows a variety of different effects.

Great care must be taken to give reverence and respect to
the altar because "at the altar the sacrifice of the cross is made
present under the sacramental signs" (G.I.R.M. #259). Therefore the altar is never used as a table of convenience or resting
place for papers, notes, cruets, or anything else.

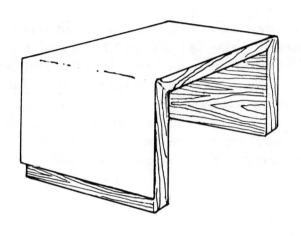

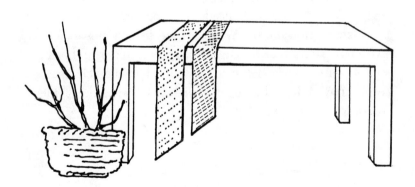

Ambo

The *ambo* (the Greek word meaning "a shelf for a book") or *lectern* (from the Latin word for "read") or the table of the Word is just that: the place for the proclamation of the Good News. It is not another good place to hang a banner. Christ is as present in the Word when it is read to the assembly as he is in the sharing of the bread and wine of Eucharist. Therefore, when the altar is enhanced with flowers and colorful textures, equal attention should be given to the ambo (G.I.R.M. #272).

Lectionary

The lectionary is the book from which the readings and Gospel are proclaimed at Mass; thus, the way the book is carried, handled, and enhanced is important. It is not appropriate to proclaim the Word of God from a missalette. The lectionary should be a large book of noble size having a strong, handsomely designed cover. It is preferable that the community design the cover, which can be made of metal, wood, leather, or needlework.

Baptistry

The baptismal font contains one of the most powerful liturgical symbols—water. Water seen, water touched, water heard! Enough water should be available for infant immersion, though the ideal is to have a pool large enough for adult immersion.

There are several areas where the baptistry—including the font, Paschal candle, oils, and space for people—can be placed. If located at the entrance to the sacred space, it has the advantage of emphasizing baptism as a rite of entrance. Here, too, the font can be used as the holy water font, reinforcing the fact that we are continually called to recommit ourselves to our baptismal promises. Also, using water from the font to sprinkle the casket at funerals is a beautiful sign symbolizing that the baptismal commitment has reached its completion. This can be done no matter where the font is located, but it is most striking here. The disadvantages of the entrance location are often insufficient space and lack of visual contact with the assembly.

Another area for the baptistry is in the midst of the assembly. Here the location speaks of baptism belonging to all and it is more visible to the assembly. Care must be taken so that the font does not block the entrance for the funeral casket or other processions.

A third possible location is near the altar. This location speaks of baptism into the "priestly people"; all share in the prayer and sacrifice of the eucharistic table. Everyone can see the action of baptism; however there may be a feeling of being separated from the assembly. No matter what location is selected, the font is both the womb of the Church and tomb in which we are buried with Christ in order to rise with him. Both demand an abundance of the symbol of water to be used liberally.

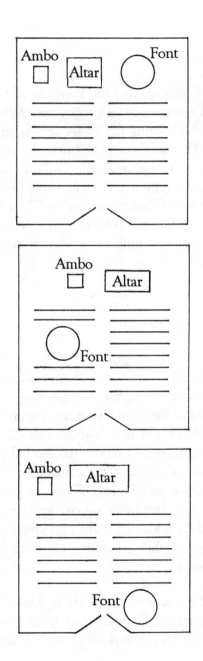

Paschal Candle

Called the Christ candle, the Easter candle, the candle of the death and resurrection of Christ, the Paschal candle is lit at the Easter vigil, during the Easter season, and at baptisms and funerals. The candle is placed near the ambo during the Easter season and placed in the baptistry at other times. During the Easter season and at funerals, the candle should have live plants and flowers around it. The community may consider making its own candle or decorating a purchased one. Always use real candles that burn down, consumed as they give light.

Oils

Oils are meant to be poured, to be smelled, and to be rubbed into the skin. Since ancient time, oil has been used in the anointing of kings and the strengthening of athletes. Jesus is the "anointed of the Lord," so it is appropriate to anoint in baptism. Today we are not familiar with oil used in these ways; all the more reason to use the symbol generously. To enhance a sense of the holy, the containers for the oils need to convey mystery and beauty. There are many interesting vases, carafes, and bottles to which carved wooden or cork stoppers could be added to make appropriate containers for the sacred oils. Another option is to commission a potter to make these vessels.

There are three sacred oils: Chrism, Oil of the Sick, and Oil of Catechumens. These oils are made from any natural plant oil; in our culture, olive oil is used. A scented oil, such

as balsam, is added to Chrism; the other two need not be scented. Chrism is used in the parish for baptism and confirmation as a sign of our sharing in the paschal mystery of Christ and being anointed with the Spirit. The bishop uses Chrism at Ordination. The anointing with the Oil of Catechumens takes place before baptism to strengthen the candidate to renounce sin and the devil. By the use of the Oil of the Sick, those who are ill are strengthened to bear suffering and receive a remedy for the illness of mind and body (Introduction to the *Rite of Blessing of Oils and Chrism*).

The Cross

When we look at the cross in our church we need to feel the impact of its message. It is a sign of death and suffering and a sign of life, hope, and resurrection. It is not necessary for everything used in church to have a cross on it. Overuse will kill the impact the cross can and should make and turn it into just another doo-dad. A central cross should be given a strong, predominate place. Other articles used in the church building should be decorated with color and design, not with crosses.

Vestments

The wearing of ritual vestments by those charged with leadership in a ritual action is an appropriate symbol of their service as well as a helpful esthetic component of the rite (E.A.C.W. #93).

Ritual vestments are clothing. They are full flowing garments. They must hang well and have dignity in their design. The presider wears these garments for all, and their dignity should tell us we are about something special. The color, design, and flow of the garments should add beauty to the environment.

Alb

The word alb means "white" and refers to the simple robe worn by both the priest and deacon. The straight-cut alb or the monk's robe-style alb are worn without a cincture or belt. There is a dignity to the strong lines of these robes, so it is appropriate that they be worn with the stole (without the chasuble) for the celebration of the sacraments of baptism, reconciliation, etc. The cinctured, light-weight, cotton, fitted alb is designed to be worn under the chasuble because it does have the dignity of design necessary for it to be worn alone. In the Eastern Rite, there is a long tradition of this "alb" or robe being the color of the chasuble.

Chasuble

The chasuble is the full circular garment designating the presider of the Mass. The medium is cloth; the folds of the garment give line; the material has texture and color expressing the liturgical season. The chasuble (the word means "little house") should be an ample garment. It is the great coat and should appear to encompass the whole assembly.

Stole

In Roman times the stole was the sign of authority. It is also reminiscent of the prayer shawl in the Jewish tradition. This three-and-a-half- to eight-inch-wide piece of material is worn over the shoulders, hanging down in the front to about mid-calf. Depending on the preference of the priest, design of the vestment, and the occasion, the stole is worn either over or under the chasuble or alone with an alb. The deacon's stole is worn over the left shoulder, across the body to the right side where the front and back are sown together at the hip.

Because the chasuble and stole are themselves the symbols, no words or so-called symbols should be added to them (E.A.C.W. #94).

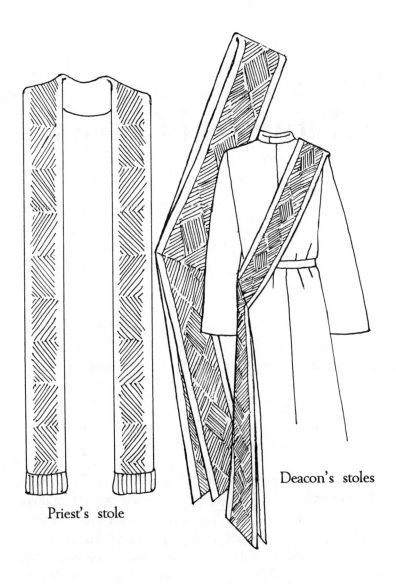

Priest's stole

Deacon's stoles

Liturgical Colors

Certain colors have been reserved for each liturgical season. These basic colors can be combined with others that complement and enhance them, thereby better capturing the "feel" of the season.

Advent/Christmas

Advent is the promise and Christmas is the fulfillment. There must be a flow from one to the other; one way of doing this is with color. White is the liturgical color for Christmas, and red purple, Roman or royal purple, plum, fuscia, or pink are the traditional colors of Advent. Combining one of the Advent colors with a little gray, sand, or silver for Advent, then combining some of the fuscia or red purple colors with white for Christmas works well to provide a measure of continuity.

The use of light or royal blue for Advent is gaining popularity. Blue has a lighter, more hopeful feel, which lends itself well to the mood scripture presents during this season. The traditional colors of Advent combined with blue enhance the environment. During the Middle Ages, a deep midnight blue was listed as a color for Advent.

Keeping one shade of purple or combination of colors for Lent and another for Advent will avoid confusion between the two seasons. While penance is the lenten focus, hope is the basis of Advent.

White with gold, red, or green traditionally says Christmas, but do not limit your choice to these colors alone.

Journey from Lent to Easter

Here is the core of our faith; in these days we delve deeply into the Paschal Mystery, into the suffering, dying, and rising of Christ. There is a rhythm to these days; we are taken from depth to height to depth to height confronting the paradox of the Gospels. Although the colors and emotions of these days are different, they are all part of one journey.

When creating the environment, this journey needs to be kept in mind. One way of doing this would be to use a large wooden cross in a predominate place, such as the vestibule, throughout Lent. The same cross would be used for the veneration of the cross on Good Friday and then be "glorified" with flowers throughout the Easter season, pulling together this whole time. Another possibility is to use strong, simply designed strips of cloth of banners in purple (and a complementary color) throughout Lent, changed to red for Passion Sunday and Good Friday, then to white and gold for Easter, reminding us we can only celebrate Easter because we journey through Lent.

LENT

During Lent the liturgical color is purple. Scripture presents a strong repentance theme, calling us to the desert to strip away all that is unnecessary. The R.C.I.A. presents a journey, a time of reevaluating and searching out what faith means to us as individuals and as a community. Strong, deep colors seem to express this season: deep blue, brown, wine, or gray combined with purple.

For Passion or Palm Sunday, the color is red.

THE TRIDUUM

Though the services are long, they demand to be celebrated in an unhurried manner. The manner in which liturgy is celebrated is more important in creating a prayerful environment than any color.

Holy Thursday: The Mass of the Lord's Supper, with its strong service focus, starts on a jubilant note and ends on a sober one with the stripping of the altar. The color of the day is white.

Good Friday: The color is red. Good Friday is the only day the Church does not celebrate Mass, and so we fast from our eucharistic meal. For the Good Friday service (there is only one service on this day), the Sacramentary notes that the deacon and priest wear "Mass vestments" (Instruction in the Roman Missal #4). The stark and simple nature of the service suggests an alb and red stole be the appropriate vestments.

The main focus is on the cross, not a crucifix. Since multiplication of symbols weakens them, only one large, rough, wooden cross should be used for all to venerate.

Easter Vigil: This is the high point of the liturgical year! The color is white, the celebration is baptism. This is the night of the primal symbols of water, fire, story, light and darkness, anointing, the sharing of bread and wine. On this night these symbols *must* be present in abundance and used liberally. If the parish celebration is minimal, work on improving one symbol/ritual action this year, adding another next year, etc. Educate the parish on what to expect and the value of the night. This is the Easter Vigil, not simply a long "anticipation Mass" for Easter Sunday.

The Great Fifty Days of Celebration

This is the celebration of resurrection and initiation. This is the time of renewal of baptismal vows, celebrations of baptism at Sunday Eucharist, First Communions, and Confirmation. When planning the flowers for the environment, budget to replace the flowers and plants as needed during the Fifty Days. The Paschal candle, baptismal font, ambo, and altar should be highlighted with plants and cloths.

The Gospel stories trace the disciples' gradual coming to recognize Christ and progressively understanding the meaning of the resurrection. This suggests a continued building of the environment. Consider using white for the vigil and adding color; bright Crayola rainbow colors or spring's pastels or triumphal (metallic) silver and/or gold. Build the environment up to Pentecost.

Pentecost

This is the feast of the Holy Spirit, therefore the liturgical color is red. But since it is part of and the end of Easter season, consideration must be given to how the color will be incorporated into the overall season. If white or white and silver and/or gold have been the colors of the Easter season, accents of red can be added. If the parish decided spring pastels captured the Easter season, something in the bold, bright pink (which is in the red family) may be added. Care must be taken that the colors fo not clash.

Ordinary Time

In this season, the liturgical color is green, which is the color of hope and growth. This combined with blue, yellow, or white, captures spring and summer beautifully. Beige, brown, rust, or gold combined with green says fall and winter. The seasons of nature, as well as the liturgical seasons, are a gift of the Creator and should be celebrated in the worship environment.

Feasts of Martyrs, the Cross, and the Spirit

These special feast days are found within all the seasons. The vibrant, passionate color red is the liturgical color for these feasts. Burgundy, red, or rose combined with gray, silver, pink, white, or even blue can be very striking.

Funerals

There is a tension between the joyful birth into the next life and a sad farewell to a community and family member (I.F.R. #162). The usual color is white. The joyful side can be heightened with the use of bright or triumphal colors. A more "farewell" feel can be gained by the use of beiges and pastels, gray, or even a touch of white and black. Usually these colors are carried out in the vestments and pall.

The pall is the white cloth placed over the coffin when it is brought into the church. The priest sprinkles the coffin with holy water, saying, "In the waters of baptism N. died with Christ and rose with him to new life. May he/she now share with him eternal glory" *(Order of Christian Funerals)*. The pall

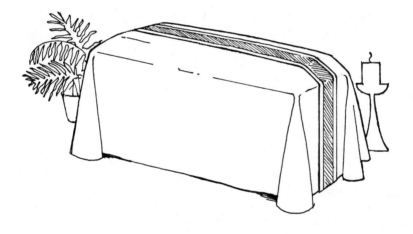

is then placed on the coffin by family members or friends. As the prayer suggests, the pall is the symbol of "putting on Christ" as in baptism. Since it is the symbol, no words or so-called "Christian symbols" are added to the pall. The simple use of color and line will enhance this garment with dignity. A clean, pressed pall, folded so it can be opened over the coffin with reverence, speaks of the respect the community has for its deceased brothers and sisters.

Making a
Sacred Space

The Artist

There is talent in your parish. There are decorators, people who sew, flower arrangers, potters, metal welders, weavers, artists, and many more. Since they are often lacking in liturgical awareness, provide training and encouragement for them.

When a liturgical object needs to be purchased, do *not* go to the catalogue. Look to the community of liturgical artists and craftspersons. Many parishes believe having sacred objects fashioned by artists is too expensive. Yet many times local artists can produce objects of a greater beauty, appropriateness, and quality at a cost very comparable or below items mass produced. Plan on paying a just fee.

"None (no liturgical furnishings) should be made in such a way that it is far removed from the print of the human hand and human craft" (E.A.C.W. #76). What do handmade chalices, altars, altar cloths, chasubles, lectionary covers, etc., say? They speak of an individual's concern for the stewardship of nature and the nurture of a community. They speak of people sharing faith with each other in the "language" they know best. This is not a frill in the worship experience. It is the substance of worship, for "people have only their own arts and styles of expression with which to celebrate" (E.A.C.W. #4).

Authenticity

Everything used in the liturgy and sacred space should be real: real plants, real candles, real flowers. Nothing phony or false has a place in an assembly of those who struggle to live authentically.

Seasonal, natural vegetation may be used in addition to the use of plants and flowers in the sacred space. Weed arrangements might be used in the fall, and pine and bare branches in winter. Driftwood, rocks, and cactus give a desert feel to Lent; bare branches give a stripped and barren look; pussy willows and forced branches speak of new life, spring, and the waters of baptism—a possible lenten environment.

Consider what *could* be done as well as how things *should* be done. Within these guidelines there is a wealth of possibilities and ideas! Every environment does not look the same. There isn't one right way for Easter to look, nor should

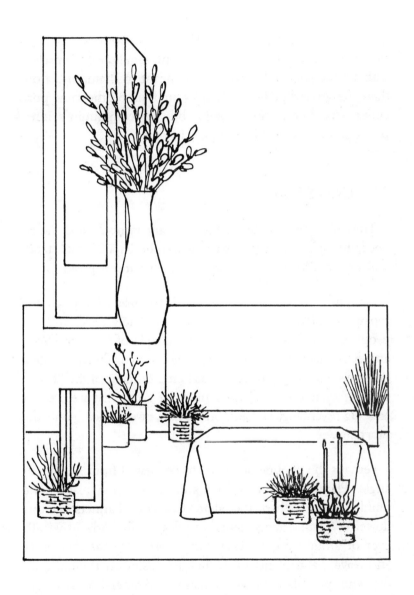

all funeral palls look the same. The liturgy planners should go to the scriptures of the season or event, familiarize themselves with its theology, ask what is has meant to them, and from there design and plan. All liturgies are built on the same principles, guidelines, and theology, but the community's interpretation of these will be uniquely its own.

The Use of Space

The assembly is one of the primary symbols and much needs to be made of the space where the baptized sit, stand, and gather. The need to be creative in this area is great!

Communion rails were removed because they created a separation of the sacred space into the "holy area" and the people's area. The gathering of the people of God for Word and Sacrament is what makes a space sacred, therefore attention needs to be given to the total environment of the "house of the people of God." Care must be taken that we are not creating psychological communion rails by enhancing only the sanctuary.

Perhaps the celebration needs to be viewed from a different angle. Planners could begin planning with the rear of the building rather than the altar. Consider banners, cloths, flower or plant arrangements, candles, or the Advent wreath over or around the doorway for people to see as they enter and leave. Palm plants might line the aisles on Passion Sunday and pine boughs at Christmas. Banners or strips of colored cloth might hang from walls, pillars, or ceiling. Consideration might be given to bringing the action of incensing

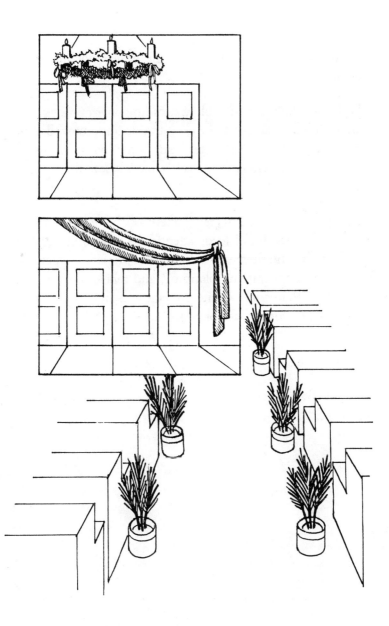

into the assembly—up and down the aisles, not just to the sanctuary step.

Is the vestibule a hospitable welcoming environment? Does it announce the season? How we gather is important. Banners lining the walkways at Easter and luminaria at Christmas speak of the festiveness of the celebration before the first note is sung.

Lighting is also an integral element of the environment. It can create a mood and focus attention. Creative use of lighting can make the theme of light and darkness an experience. This requires experiment, planning, and rehearsal in order to be effective. Remember to incorporate as many senses as possible into the liturgical celebrations (E.A.C.W. #5).

Using Art in
Sunday Worship

Part II

Design

General Principles

There are a few basic design principles that need to be kept in mind whether designing a stole or the total environment.

1. Keep it simple.

2. Never cut anything in half. Usually think of your space in thirds.

3. Usually three colors, or two colors and a trim, are more interesting. An odd number of colors is better aesthetically.

4. A symmetrical (what is on one side of the arrangement is the same on the other side) design has a comforting psychological effect. It is also easier to do. An asymmetrical arrangement is one in which something done on one side is balanced on the other

side by something different. Because it is psychologically a little unnerving, it is a challenging arrangement and also more interesting to look at. This type of arrangement, which is difficult to achieve, must still be balanced.

5. Psychologically speaking, straight lines are stronger and masculine, while curved lines are more comforting, softer, and feminine. There is a time and place for both in the environment.

6. Add interest by using different texture as well as different colors. Texture also communicates feelings, such as rough and barren or plush and full. Be sure the texture is conveying the feel of the season.

7. Bring into the design shapes from the sacred space. For example, if there are many arches in the building, occasionally use that line in a design.

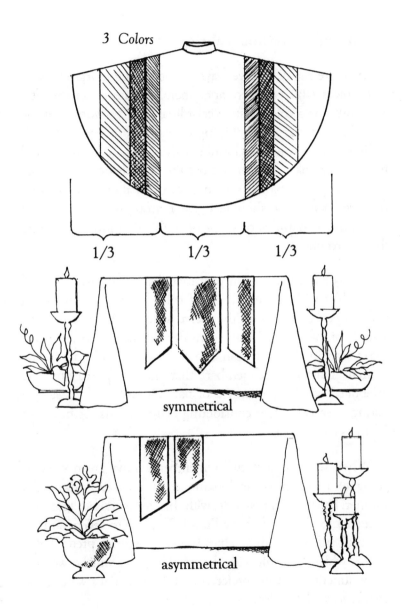

3 Colors

1/3　　　1/3　　　1/3

symmetrical

asymmetrical

Choice of Color and Fabric

There are many creative ways of combining liturgical colors with colors which will enhance them. A runner on the altar and ambo or a colored stole coordinated to be worn over the chasuble is a way of combining colors. Another possibility is to line and/or trim the chasuble either at the edge or around the neck or yoke. This brings out the circular lines of the garment. Strips of colored material sewn on the chasuble from front to back at the shoulders give a strong masculine line to the garment. Banners or strips of cloth bring more color into the environment.

Be aware of the colors in your sacred space, in the walls and rugs. How will a given shade of color go with them? What will happen to a color in the sacred space? Ask the store for a sample of the material being considered because a color which looks fine in the store can can look totally different in the church building. Remember that liturgical seasons are celebrated within the context of natural seasons. Be aware of nature's seasons when considering plants, weeds, or branches for the sacred space.

When selecting material, remember a heavy green velvet is going to make everyone looking at in on a 90° day a lot warmer!The presider stands with his arms raised and outstretched for the Eucharistic Prayer. The five to seven yards of material necessary for a chasuble can become pretty heavy after a while. Consult with the presider who will be wearing the vestment about his preference of the material's weight and texture as well as color.

Chasuble Patterns

In order to assist the parish in designing a chasuble of beauty and dignity, the following measurements for making a vestment are offered. Please note the difference in fullness in the three chasuble cuts: bishop cut, full cut, and the great coat cut. The required amount of material is noted on each design. In order for the vestment to hang evenly when it is worn, it is necessary to cut the back three inches longer than the front.

Directions for Cutting a Chasuble Pattern

1. Measure and cut the pattern out of an old sheet or a paper or plastic tablecloth.

2. Enlarge the neck facing patterns found on page 58 as the guide to cut the neck opening. Use the edge indicated on that pattern. There is a 1/2" seam allowance.

3. In order to get the arch of the curve of the vestment right, take a piece of string the length of the vertical measurement (from the shoulder to the bottom—on bishop cut, these are 53" and 56"), tie a piece of chalk on one end, and pin the other end to the top corner. Using this as a compass, make the arch. The shoulder seam allowance is ¾" to 1 inch. Roll the hem and either machine or hand stitch, depending on the material. Any non-stretch material that hangs well is appropriate for a chasuble.

Pin string with chalk ↗

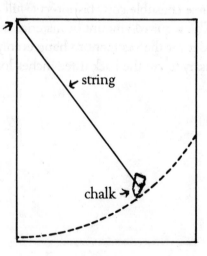

string

chalk →

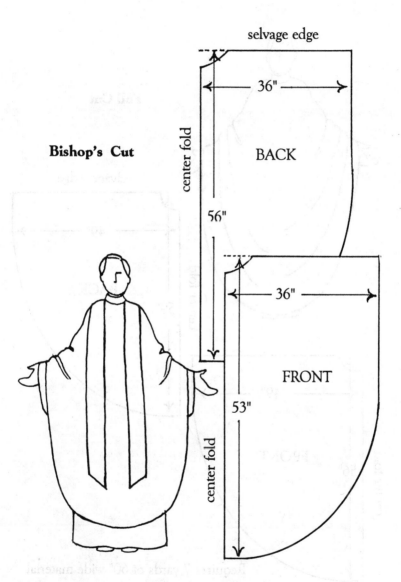

Bishop's Cut

selvage edge

center fold

36"

BACK

56"

center fold

36"

FRONT

53"

center fold

Requires 5 yards of 60" wide material

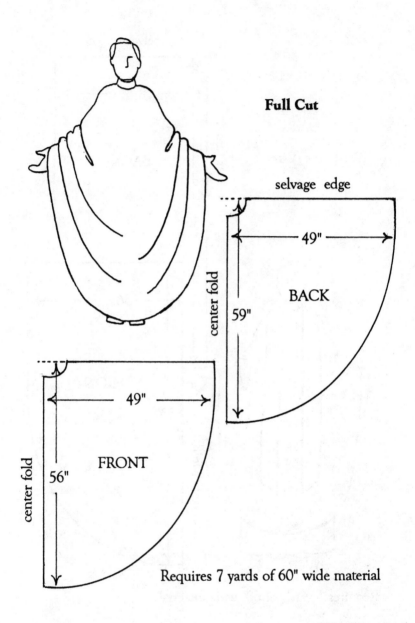

Full Cut

selvage edge

← 49" →

center fold

BACK

59"

← 49" →

center fold

FRONT

56"

Requires 7 yards of 60" wide material

Great Coat Cut

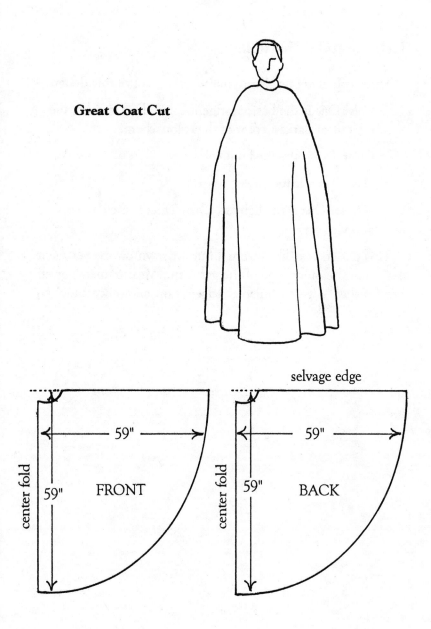

Hebrew-style Chasuble

Three colors are needed to make a vestment of this design.

Color One is the basic vestment color. This is either the lightest or darkest color of the color scheme.

Color Two is the medium color.

Color Three is the accent color.

If *Color One* is the lightest, *Color Three* is the darkest, and vice versa.

This design is either inserted into or sewn on the vestment 10" from the outer edge of the garment. (Measurements given are finished edge to finished edge; seam allowance must be added.)

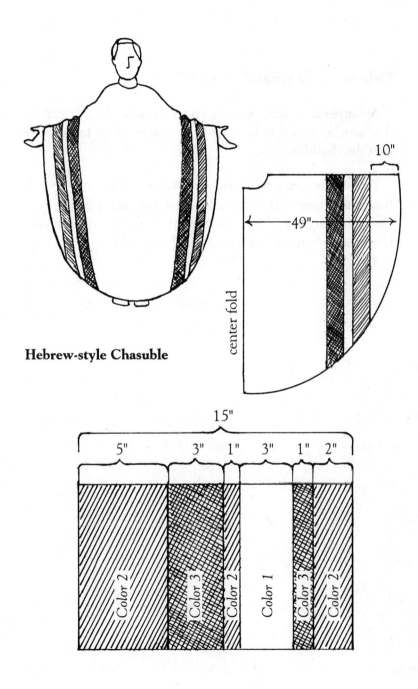

10"

49"

center fold

Hebrew-style Chasuble

15"

5"   3"   1"   3"   1"   2"

Color 2

Color 3

Color 2

Color 1

Color 3

Color 2

Hebrew-style Chasuble with Stole

A simple stole can be worn under the chasuble, or part of the "arm" design may be adapted to a stole design to be worn over the chasuble.

This design may be varied by placing the insert 7" to 9" from the center of the chasuble. Mark the center by pressing along the center fold and measure from there. For this vestment the stole must be worn under the chasuble.

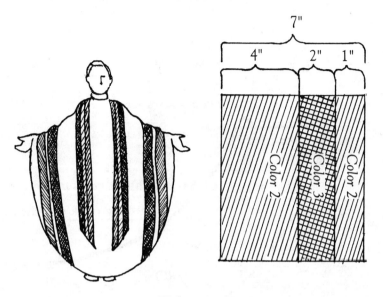

7"

4"   2"   1"

Color 2   Color 3   Color 2

Hebrew-style Chasuble with Stole

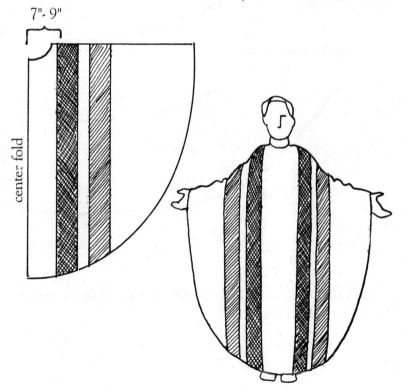

7"- 9"

center fold

Facing Patterns

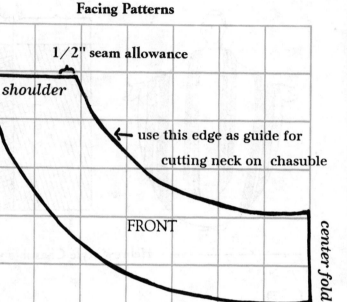

Each square equals 1". Use pattern to cut out facing as you would for a dress neck.

Stole Designs

Stole to be Worn under the Chasuble

To make the pattern:

1. Enlarge the patterns (found on pages 61-62). Note the seam allowance of ½" has been added to the pattern pieces.

2. Place the top pattern piece on a piece of palon or trace-a-pattern.

3. Measure from the shoulder line to where the bottom of the stole will come on the priest from whom you are making it. (The stole should hang to the middle of the priest's calf.)

4. Once you have measured to where the bottom of the stole will be, put the bottom stole pattern piece in place.

5. Draw a line to join the two pattern pieces. Note the stole is narrow at the neck and shoulder and becomes wider at the bottom.

6. Now you have a pattern for a stole that hangs nicely and can be comfortably worn under the chasuble.

To make the stole:

1. Cut out two pieces of material for the front side of the stole and join them at the center-back seam.

2. Cut out two pieces of material for the stole lining and join them at the center-back seam.

3. With wrong sides together, sew the front side to the lining, allowing a ½" seam.

4. Leave the bottom open on one side of the stole for turning.

5. Turn right side out and press.

6. Slip stitch the open bottom closed.

7. Top stitch all the way around the stole.

Each square equals 1".

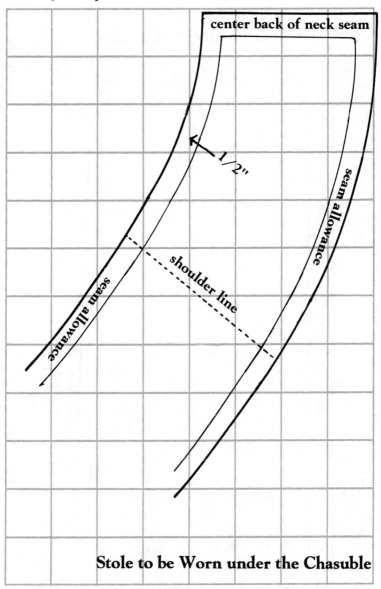

center back of neck seam

seam allowance

1/2"

shoulder line

seam allowance

Stole to be Worn under the Chasuble

Each square equals 1".

Stole to be Worn under the Chasuble

seam allowance

seam allowance

← 1/2"

bottom of stole

Stole to be Worn over the Chasuble

To make the pattern:

1. Enlarge the patterns (found on pages 65-66). Note the seam allowance of ½" has been added to the pattern pieces.

2. Place the top pattern piece on a piece of palon or trace-a-pattern.

3. Measure from the shoulder line to where the bottom of the stole will come on the priest from whom you are making this. (Three to four inches from the bottom of the chasuble.)

4. Once you have measured to where the bottom of the stole will be, put the bottom stole pattern piece in place.

5. Draw a line to join the two pattern pieces. Note the stole is narrow at the neck and shoulder and becomes wider at the bottom.

6. Now you have a pattern for a stole that hangs nicely and can be worn under a chasuble or alb.

To make to stole:

1. Cut out two pieces of material for the front side of the stole and join them at the center-back seam.

2. Cut out two pieces of material for the stole lining and join them at the center-back seam.

3. With wrong sides together, sew the front side to the lining, allowing a ½" seam.

4. Leave the bottom open on one side of the stole for turning.

5. Turn right side out and press.

6. Slip stitch the open bottom closed.

7. Top stitch all the way around the stole.

Each square equals 1".

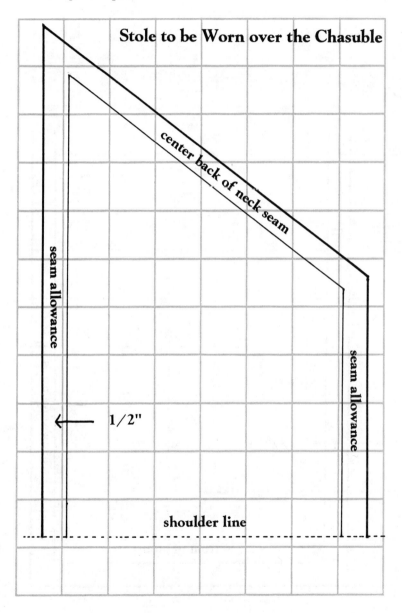

Stole to be Worn over the Chasuble

center back of neck seam

seam allowance

seam allowance

1/2"

shoulder line

Each square equals 1".

Stole to be Worn over the Chasuble

seam allowance

seam allowance

← 1/2"

bottom of stole

Banners

The purpose of banners is to focus attention and create a mood, *not* to state a theme, bear a slogan, or teach. Banner designs should be simple, enhancing the mood of the season or event.

Banners might also be strips of colored cloth, either of a heavy, stately material or a light, breezy cloth, depending on the mood desired. These are either carried in procession or stationed beforehand. When banners are carried in procession, care must be taken that the back is finished, either lined or, if the wrong side of the material is attractive, edges may be roll hemmed.

Banners made of red and white material, fluttering over the heads of the assembly as they are carried during the entrance procession, capture and set the mood for the celebration of Pentecost in a way words on a banner never could. Be sure banners are large enough to fit the space you are putting them in. Most churches have high ceilings and wonderful wall space, so think big.

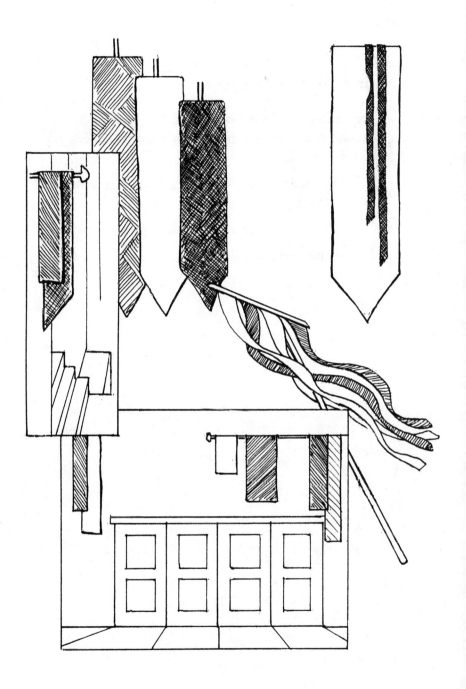

Cutting a Banner Design

This banner measured eleven feet. Five pairs of banners were hung on the side walls for the Easter season.

1. For the background choose a medium to heavyweight *colored* material.

2. Cut the filigree design from a heavy palon.

3. Place the palon over the drawn design and trace.

Constructing a Banner Stand with Base

This banner stand and base is lightweight and strong. It is excellent for carrying in procession.

1. The stand is made of 1" x 1" fir stripping joined at a tee at the top.

2. The base is made of 1" x 4" pine boards joined as the diagram shows.

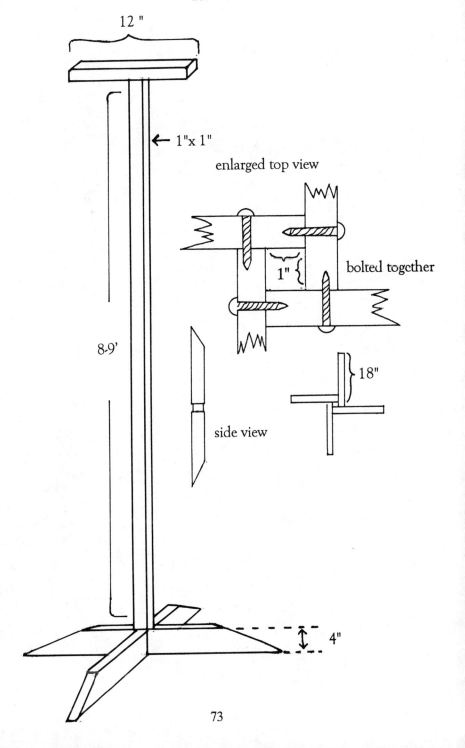

12 "

← 1"x 1"

enlarged top view

bolted together

1"

8-9'

side view

18"

4"

Bibliography

Adam, Adol. *The Liturgical Year.* New York: Pueblo Publishing Co., 1981.

Constitution on the Sacred Liturgy. Chicago: Liturgy Training Publications, 1963.

Environment and Art in Catholic Worship. Chicago: Liturgy Training Publications, 1978.

General Instruction of the Roman Missal. Chicago: Liturgy Training Publications, 1975.

General Norms for the Liturgical Year and the Calendar. Chicago: Liturgy Training Publications, 1969.

Hovda, Robert. *Dry Bones.* Washington, D.C.: The Liturgical Conference, 1973.

Huck, Gabe. *Liturgy with Style and Grace.* Chicago: Liturgy Training Publications, 1978.

Introduction of the Funeral Rite. New York: Pueblo Publishing Co., 1969.

Kavanagh, Aidan. *Elements of Rite.* New York: Pueblo Publishing Co., 1982.

Keifer, Ralph A. *Blessed and Broken.* Wilmington, Delaware: Michael Glazier, 1982.

_____. *To Give Thanks and Praise.* Washington, D.C.: National Association of Pastoral Musicians, 1980.

Martos, Joseph. *Doors to the Sacred.* Garden City, N.Y.: Image Books, 1982.

Mitchell, Nathan, OSB. *Cult and Controversy: The Worship of the Eucharist Outside of Mass.* New York: Pueblo Publishing Co., 1982.

Ostdiek, Gilbert. *Catechesis for Liturgy.* Washington, D.C.: The Pastoral Press, 1986.

Owen, David G. *Transparent Worship.* United Methodist Church: Education and Cultivation Division, 1979.

White, James F. *Introduction to Christian Worship.* Nashville: Abingdon Press, 1980.

INCLUDE THE ARTS IN YOUR PLANNING WITH MODERN LITURGY

MODERN LITURGY
for the Artist and Planner

Modern Liturgy is the only liturgical resource devoted to planning worship with help from all of the arts. If you're trying to blend the musical, lively, and environmental arts into your parish worship, this is your magazine! Every issue contains ideas for dramas, stories, gestures, songs, decoration, and design — all in plenty of time for your seasonal planning. Make it easy on yourself: Get a subscription today!

One year (ten issues): $40

Order Form -

Send this order form to:
Modern Liturgy, 160 E. Virginia St., #290, San Jose, CA 95112.

☐ Yes, I would like to start receiving the creative ideas of top liturgists from around the world. Rush me my first issue of *Modern Liturgy* and reserve my one-year subscription (10 issues for $40.00). If I'm not satisfied, I can return the invoice marked "Cancel" and *keep my first issue free.*

Name: _____

Institution: _____

Address: _____

City/State/Zip: _____

Code: UAS

Save Time and Energy with These Planning Resources

 **The Modern Liturgy Planning Guide** *by Robert Zappulla, et al.* A great planning resource for liturgists! You'll receive a Scripture commentary, idea starters, and music suggestions for every Sunday of Cycles A, B, and C of the Roman lectionary. There are also seasonal comments and suggestions in this workbook so that you can retain your notes for the next cycle. Paperbound, $19.95, ISBN 0-89390-088-5

 **The Word and Eucharist Handbook** *by Lawrence J. Johnson.* A reference guide to the Liturgy of the Word and the Liturgy of the Eucharist. Designed especially for worship planners, ministers, and liturgical artists, use it to answer your questions about the origin, development, and modern practice of each part of the Mass. Paperbound, $9.95, ISBN 0-89390-067-2

 **In the Potter's Hand** *by Robert Eimer OMI and Sarah O'Malley OSB.* These scripture-based wake services provide more flexibility, broader choices, and greater personalization, which allow bereaved family members to get more out of the service. Each service is centered on a symbol and the symbol is reflected in the readings, psalms, and prayers. Paperbound, $6.95, ISBN 0-89390-132-6

 **The Holy Week Book** *edited by Eileen E. Freeman.* Plan more creative Holy Week liturgies with this important resource. It provides historical background, liturgical theology, creative ideas, and more than 60 practical presentations on Palm Sunday, Holy Thursday, Good Friday, and the Easter Vigil. Includes: Palm Sunday parade, Passover Seder ideas, build-it-yourself cross for Good Friday, children's celebrations, and decorating ideas. Paperbound, $19.95, ISBN 0-89390-007-9

 **Come, Let Us Celebrate! Creative Reconciliation Services** *by Robert Eimer, OMI, and Sarah O'Malley, OSB.* These sixteen services are adaptable for Rites II and III of the Roman Catholic sacrament of penance. Each has symbols and themes carried out in the prayers, homily, examination, scripture readings, and songs. The book also includes twelve ideas that can be used to create additional services. Paperbound, $9.95, ISBN 0-89390-082-6

Order these books from your local bookstore, or complete the order form on the last page.

Environment Resources

It's a Banner Year!
by George Collopy
Paperbound $11.95, 230 pages, 6" x 9", ISBN 0-89390-176-8
If you're looking for fresh banner ideas, or fresh ways to hang them, you'll love these patterns from the award-winning art director of *Modern Liturgy* magazine. More than 100 banner and temporary-art designs for liturgical seasons, sacraments, and secular holidays. Designs have grid overlays for easy reproduction.

Banners Without Words
by Jill Knuth
Paperbound $10.95, 198 pages, 6" x 9", ISBN 0-89390-075-3
This collection of design ideas, illustrations, instructions, and handy tips will help you make your own beautiful, wordless banners. More than 50 reproducible designs!

Banners and Such
by Adelaide Ortegel, SP
Paperbound $10.95, 127 pages, 7" x 10", ISBN 0-89390-092-3
A basic source of design principles for any visual construction—banners, altar cloths, vestments, antependiums, and other creative visual articles. Revised edition includes new section on environments and updated resource guide.

Light: Multimedia Techniques for Celebration
by Adelaide Ortegel, SP
Paperbound $10.95, 127 pages, 7" x 10", ISBN 0-89390-094-X
Light up your next gathering! All you need is a slide projector or overhead—and *Light: Multimedia Techniques for Celebration*. Learn how to make your own slides out of paint, acetate, or contact paper, how to create wonderful fluid effects with an overhead, how to use dissolve techniques, and how to operate two or more projectors at the same time.

Symbols for All Seasons:
Planning Worship Environments for Cycles A, B, and C
by Cathrine H. Krier
Paperbound $9.95, 175 pages, 5 1/2" x 8 1/2", ISBN 0-89390-125-3
Chock-full of symbols based on the Sunday lectionary readings for all three cycles, this book also gives you tips on liturgy planning, artistic considerations, and color. Includes space to jot down your own ideas.

Ask for these books at your local dealer, or complete the order form on the last page.

Other Art Ideas

Clip Art for Bulletins and Beyond
by George F. Collopy
Paperbound $14.95, 144 perforated pages, 8 1/2" x 11"
ISBN 0-89390-124-5
Produce easy-to-do, eye-pleasing bulletins, banners, and programs with art appropriate for any Sunday of the liturgical year and in various sizes for your convenience. Learn how to use clip art to your best advantage, how to make different bulletins using different folds, and how to enlarge the art to your specifications.

Clip Art for Communicating the Good News
by Jean Morningstar
Paperbound $14.95, 128 perforated pages, 8 1/2" x 11"
ISBN 0-89390-160-1
Enhance your printed message with this original clip art. These drawings illustrate passages from the Bible, and they cover the seasons of Advent, Christmas, Lent, Easter, Pentecost, and many other feasts. The unique format allows you to use them "as is" or in your own designs. Great for stationery, newsletters, student handouts, Sunday bulletins, and flyers.

"The artistic drawings and calligraphy of Sr. Jean Morningstar are a wonderful blend of simplicity and inspiration. I have used her work in school newsletters, invitations, liturgical program booklets, and stationery. . .in all cases her work is striking and adds greatly to the material." —Br. Frederick Dihlmann, FSC, St. Joseph's Collegiate Institute, Buffalo, NY